W9-AYR-774

J   5585450
796.93   16.95
Rog
Rogers
Skiing

DATE DUE		
MY 12 '05		

AL

AL

GAYLORD MG

SKIING

WRITTEN BY HAL ROGERS

ROURKE CORPORATION, INC.
VERO BEACH, FLORIDA 32964

PRO-AM SPORTS

The Rourke Corporation, Inc.
P.O. Box 3328, Vero Beach, FL 32964

Rogers, Hal 1966—
    Skiing / by Hal Rogers.
      p. cm. — (Pro-am sports)
    Includes bibliographical references (p. 47)
    ISBN 0-86593-348-0
    1. Skills and skiing—Juvenile literature. I. Title.
II. Series.
    GV854.R64 1993
    796.93—dc20   93-23410
                                    CIP
                                     AC

Cover photograph: Jack M. Affleck
Interior Photographs:
Jack M. Affleck 7, 26, 28, 36, 39, 41
Allsport USA 32 (Guido Benetton/Agence Vandystadt),
    33 (Ian Tomlinson), 35 (Jean-Marc Barey/Agence
    Vandystadt), 38 (Sylvie Chappaz/Agence
    Vandystadt)
Aspen Skiing Company 4 (Henrik Kam); 9 (Aaron
    Strong); 16, 17, 43 (Team Russell); 21 (Hal
    Williams); 31 (John Bing)
Colorado Ski Country USA 5 (T.R. Youngstrom/Telluride
    Ski Resort); 10, 14 (Monarch Ski Resort); 12 (Tom
    Johnson/Telluride Ski Resort); 20 (Nathan
    Bilow/Monarch Ski Resort); 25 (Grafton
    Smith/Telluride Ski Resort)

Series Editor: Gregory Lee
Book design and production:
    The Creative Spark, San Clemente, CA

Printed in the USA

SKIING

The exhilaration of flying down wintry white slopes has turned millions of people into ski lovers.

CONTENTS

HOT TIP:
Want to learn how to turn on skis? See page 23.

To ski lovers, a slope covered with fresh powder is one of the finest sights on Earth.

Powder, Speed, Bumps, and Jumps

You're about to take your first run of the day. The chair lift hardly seems to move—you can't wait to hit the slopes. The weather is surprisingly warm. It snowed last night, leaving a perfect layer of powder to try. Only two or three skiers have left their tracks in the fresh snow—there's still plenty of untouched powder waiting. Finally, the end of the lift is in sight. It's time to get your skis moving.

Once off the lift, you slip your pole straps over your gloved wrists and look around. The view is incredible, and the mountains seem to go on forever. You admire the scene for a moment, but your skis seem to have a mind of their own. All of a sudden, you find yourself looking down a monster run. There aren't any moguls on this one—you'll save the bumps for later. But there's a steep drop and some tasty powder.

Sometimes the powder is so plentiful that your skis whip up mounds of it.

The first run of any ski day is always a little scary. You haven't tested the snow yet. "Can I do it?" you wonder, looking down a hill that seems to get steeper and steeper. Nothing to do but to try. You're off.

You move across the mountain for a few seconds, getting the feel of the snow before starting a serious descent. The powder is deep enough that the skis sink below the surface. You can't see them, but it doesn't matter. You keep your eyes straight ahead. The faster you go, the easier it is to make turns. Good thing you learned a few new tricks about skiing on powder during your last lesson.

Before you know it, the run is over, and you're making your way back to the chair lift. A few more people have come out to enjoy the day. This time, you'll go further up the mountain, keeping ahead of the crowds for a little while longer. Today may be your best day of skiing yet.

Sounds great, doesn't it? It could happen, even if you've never been on a pair of skis. Skiing is an easy sport to learn, and it only takes dedication and interest to become a good skier. Beginners find that after just one morning of lessons with a capable instructor, they are able to make it down easy hills. Becoming an expert takes a lot more time and effort, but for most skiers, it isn't work—it's fun and excitement.

Spending a day on skis is the favorite pastime of more than 15 million Americans and Canadians. Some of these skiers are experts who spend their winters competing in international championships. Others simply have fun edging their way down the intermediate and beginner slopes. Skiing is great fun at any age and at any skill level. Maybe that's why the sport has been around for so long.

History

People have been skiing for thousands of years, but for most of that time, skiing was considered a form of transportation, not a sport. In Europe and Asia, people who lived in cold, snowy climates used long and narrow runners to glide across the snow. Early skis were quite long, often up to 14 feet, because they kept skiers from falling waist-deep into fresh, powdery snow. Travel on skis was quicker than walking, or even using snowshoes, because it enabled people to slide easily across the top of the snow instead of sinking into it.

Using skis to travel from one place to another is still popular, but today people do it mostly for fun, not out of necessity. This kind of skiing is called *Nordic skiing* because the Norwegians were the first to do it—and the first to recognize that it could be fun! Also called *cross-country skiing*, Nordic skiers glide across flat or slightly hilly terrain. Cross-country skiers often travel over great distances, much like their early predecessors.

Cross-country skiing is like hiking on skis. It is easy to learn, but you have to be in good shape to keep up the pace. Imagine spending the day gliding

Nordic or cross-country skiers enjoy an entirely different experience from downhill skiing.

through snow-covered fields, climbing up and coasting down little hills, and pushing your way across a flat, white meadow. It takes a lot of energy and stamina.

Nordic skiers use two different techniques to move across the landscape. The first, called the *diagonal stride*, looks a little like jogging on skis. The skier leans slightly over the front of the skis, moving one ski forward and then the other, shifting the weight back and forth between the two skis. The ski poles are set in the snow and pushed backward to help the skier move forward.

The other basic move in cross-country skiing is the *skate*. Here, one ski glides forward in a straight line, while the other is kicked out sideways and back in a skating motion. This looks much like the movement a skater makes to propel his or her body across the ice.

Alpine Skiing

Alpine skiing, or skiing downhill, originated late in the nineteenth century in Austria. The name comes from the Alps, the European mountain system where downhillers first challenged the *fall line* (the direct, straight-down route to the bottom of a hill). If you were to roll a ball down a mountain, it would follow the fall line—and gain speed as it moved downward.

Skiing straight down a hill without turning or stopping is called *straight running* or *schussing*, and this builds up speed very quickly. Downhill skiers realized long ago that they would have to find ways to slow down when they were going too fast. *Traversing* is one way of doing this. Traversing is skiing at a 90-degree angle to the fall line, that is, across the mountain. Turning is another way to slow down, but many consider it to be the most difficult part of downhill skiing. There are many different kinds of ski turns, from the relatively easy *wedge* or snowplow to the difficult *carved parallel*.

Braving the Mountains

Well into the twentieth century, skiing continued to be an important way for people to get around in snowy places that were otherwise unpassable. For example, ski patrols were used in the mountains of Finland to stop the Soviet military from invading that country during World War II. The United States Army also used ski troops to fight the German military in the Italian mountains.

Skiers learn to cross a slope by zig-zagging. This is known as traversing downhill.

Fortunately, however, skiing became more than just a way to cross harsh, snowy regions. It turned into a major sport.

As skiers around the world began to invent better ways to move across the mountains and valleys on skis, more people thought they should give it a try. By the 1920s, skiing had become so popular that Nordic competition was part of the very first Winter Olympic Games. Alpine events followed in the 1936 Olympics. Ski lifts were invented in the 1930s, and downhill skiers no longer had to climb up a hill for the thrill of going down it. Thousands of people tried Alpine skiing—and loved it. The first ski lift, a rope tow at Shawbridge, Quebec, cost a nickel per ride.

By the late 1940s, inventors had even learned how to manufacture snow. Dry spells were no longer a problem, and people could start skiing earlier in the season than ever before. Today, many ski areas depend on snow-making machines to keep the slopes safer and more fun.

Technological advances attracted attention to the sport, but winners of important ski events also caused a stir. Olympic medalists like American Gretchen Fraser and Norwegian Stein Eriksen captured the interest of spectators around the world in the 1940s and '50s. When Eriksen immigrated to the United States, his dashing looks, unusual skiing style, and spectacular airborne somersaults made everyone want to give the sport a try. Jean-Claude Killy, the superstar of the 1960s, caught the world's eye when he won the World Cup in 1967 and then garnered three Olympic gold medals a year later.

These superb athletes brought glamour and excitement to the sport. Soon the lure of the slopes became too strong to resist, and new skiers began leaving their tracks on slopes across Europe and North America. New ski resorts appeared, and people traveled many miles to take on the most famous slopes in the world, like those of Aspen, Colorado, and St. Moritz, Switzerland.

Expert skiers are always looking for new, more challenging ski runs to test their abilities.

Many people were happy to enjoy occasional visits to their favorite ski areas and ski for fun whenever they got the chance. Others became champions—some in real competition, others by skiing in places that most people would consider impossible. Before long, *Freestyle skiing* became a new way of attacking the snow. These daredevils who enjoy "hot dogging" perform amazing stunts, seemingly learning to fly using the snow for lift off and their skis for wings.

Good skiers do not necessarily compete in international championships or race in the Olympics; many are content to compete only against themselves. There is glory not only in winning a medal, but in sharpening skills and testing your limits. For those who love the sport, competition is not always an international race. It may be perfecting a 180-degree helicopter off a five-foot *mogul*, or simply progressing from the easy slopes to the intermediates. Whether one's goal is to cut through the gates of a slalom course or just learn to parallel ski, all levels of skiers share one thing: love for the sport.

With enough practice, anyone can participate in races, thrash down the slopes at high speeds, careen over cliffs into daring vertical leaps, or swim downhill in powder that seems to be knee-deep. Surprisingly enough, all these things can be done without risk. All it takes is knowledge and skill—and hours of preparation. It won't happen overnight, but with enough miles on the slopes comes advanced skiing. Many skiers, of course, just want to have fun flying down hills or trekking through forests with their friends. That's even easier to accomplish.

Whatever your goals, you need the right equipment and training before you can hit the ground skiing. It may take a lot of work to become a good skier, but the best part is you will have fun doing it!

Y ou're never too young to learn to ski. All you need is desire.

Before You Go

"I was 14 the first time I went skiing," says Vermont native Mitch. "The only reason I went was because everyone I knew skied, and I felt like I was missing out on the fun."

Mitch's first experience on skis wasn't great. First of all, he hadn't done anything athletic since baseball season the summer before. Second, he didn't have any of the right gear. Third, he decided to ski with his friends instead of taking a lesson.

"I borrowed my Dad's old skis and boots. They were from the '70s and in pretty bad shape. Plus, the boots were way too big. It took me 15 minutes to put my skis on. All my friends were getting impatient. Then they decided to be nice to me and take me on an easy slope first. Unfortunately, their idea of easy was a lot different than mine. Even the ride up the lift was hard."

Mitch fell getting off the chairlift, so his jeans were wet from the very start. "I fell so often they didn't get a chance to dry!" he remembers. His feet were freezing before he made it down the first run—not surprising, since it took him a lot longer than any of his friends. After just one run, one friend showed him to the easiest slope on the mountain, and everyone else left for the bigger runs.

After two or three more runs, Mitch was cold and tired. His ankles hurt, and he was getting a blister on his heel. Then he fell and twisted his ankle. "My skis were way too long for a first-timer, and I didn't have a clue what I was doing. I'm lucky that nothing worse happened."

A year after his disastrous first try, Mitch's family took a weekend trip to a popular ski resort. His parents insisted he rent proper equipment and take a lesson. "This time, I liked the sport immediately. We bought some warm clothes, I was learning how to handle the slopes, and skiing seemed like the coolest sport in the world." Today Mitch likes to ski intermediate runs and hits the slopes at least one or two days each month of the ski season.

Mitch's story isn't unusual—except that he tried the sport again after a really unpleasant first experience. Those who go skiing without any preparation wonder what so many people see in it. The best way to keep this from happening is to find out what you need to have a successful first day on the slopes.

Fitness and Skiing

No skier will tell you that skiing is easy on your body. In fact, a typical remark from a first-time skier is, "I used muscles I didn't even know I had!"

To enjoy skiing it's important to be physically fit. Your muscles will really get a workout when you ski for the first time.

Skis are designed to help you get down a mountain and to help you turn, but it takes muscular effort to accomplish this.

There are two very good reasons why you should be in shape before you start skiing. First, beginners who are in good physical condition learn to ski much faster than those who are not. In fact, once skiers reach a certain level of excellence, the only way they can improve is to become physically stronger. Second, skiers who are in good condition are injured much less frequently than those who are not. You can protect various parts of the body, including joints and ligaments, by developing your muscles.

Does this mean you have to be a world-class athlete to be a successful skier? Not at all. People of all shapes and sizes can do well. What's important is that you achieve the best state of fitness you can before heading out to the slopes. So how do you get fit? *Conditioning*, or exercising to get or stay in shape, is a vital step to achieving success at any sport.

Most forms of exercise help you build physical strength or stamina. Stamina and endurance are particularly important for Nordic skiing, a sport that demands that you be able to push yourself over long periods of time. A good way to build stamina is by jogging or doing aerobics. Both of these activities increase your cardiovascular fitness, or the strength and health of your heart and lungs. Jogging and aerobics will also strengthen your muscles so that your body can keep moving all day.

Downhill skiers also need to be in good shape, but gravity does give them a little bit of help. Instead of pushing themselves *across* a mountain, Alpine skiers guide themselves *down* it. They still need stamina, of course, but muscle strength is particularly important for the downhill skier. Muscles must be able to control the skis, pushing them to turn and respond as needed.

To build muscle strength, the fibers that build muscle have to be stimulated with work. For example, lifting weights is one way to stimulate the muscles. Weights are not for everyone, however, and should only be used under the guidance of a knowledgeable adult. Other exercises include hiking, riding a bike, and running. Specific exercises, including push-ups or wall sits (holding yourself in a seated position without a chair using a wall for balance), also strengthen muscles.

As you improve your fitness, skiing can be a fun part of your workout! You'll find that you are able to achieve more on the slopes than before. Skiers often spend six or seven hours on the slopes or cross-country trails—that's a lot of physical activity. Those who have the most success and are injured the least are the ones who don't tire quickly and who leave the slopes when they start wearing out. Only fitness can get you through an all-day workout on skis.

The Gear

Ski equipment has changed a lot over the years. For example, in the old days even beginners used extra long skis. Today, skiers usually start with skis that are shorter than they are. Most experts suggest that beginners rent skis until they are able to use longer ones, avoiding unnecessary expense when skis need to be replaced too often. Equipment, from boots to poles to skis, can be rented at many different places. There are almost always rental shops at ski areas as well as in nearby towns. If you are going to ski for several

All ski resorts rent equipment to beginners and offer instruction. Notice the length of the skis.

days, you can often get a package deal that is less expensive than renting one day at a time.

In general, the taller, heavier, and more skilled a skier is, the longer his or her skis will be. Beginners should use skis that reach from the ground to anywhere between eye level to about two inches above the head. Intermediate skiers should select skis that are about two to four inches taller than they are. When renting or buying skis, you should have the assistance of a skilled salesperson who knows which skis are right for you, as well as how tall they should be. The most knowledgeable salespeople are always skiers themselves.

You must always be honest about your skills so that the salesperson can best decide what equipment you should be using. It won't do any good to pretend that you're better than you are and end up with the wrong skis. Poorly chosen skis can slow down your progress.

Today's skis have metal edges that help skiers make turns and control speed. Modern skiers can't imagine skiing without them, but not so long ago, skiers did just that. Skis were also much less flexible, which further hampered the ability to control them. While older skis were made only of wood, manufacturers now combine many high-tech materials, such as fiber glass, plastics, and polyurethane foam with wood and metal to make skis that are both strong and functional. Skis are constructed in various ways for different types of skiing. For example, recreational skis are not the same as racing skis; Nordic skis are very different from Alpine skis.

Bindings hold the boot in place in the middle of the ski. Downhill bindings have two parts, a toe and a heel, that hold the boot securely on the ski. Nordic bindings attach only to the toe, which makes the hiking movements of cross-country skiing much easier. Most bindings are made so that you can just step into them, and they lock automatically; others need to be latched manually.

Bindings are the most important safety items in the sport. They are designed not only to hold your boot in place, but to release it in case of an emergency. Amazing as it sounds, today's bindings "sense" when you are going over the normal dips and bumps of a mountain and when you've gotten into trouble. "Smart" bindings can tell the difference between normal skiing force and abnormal force that may cause injury. If you're in danger or if you take a bad fall, a binding should release the ski from your foot smoothly and quickly. When the foot releases from the bindings, *ski brakes* grip the snow to keep the ski nearby.

Ill-fitting boots will ruin a ski experience, so many skiers believe that choosing the right boots is the most important decision you can make when buying equipment. Boots should support your feet and lower legs to help

Having the right equipment—especially skis and boots that fit properly—is essential to enjoyable skiing.

you keep your balance. In the early days of sport skiing, skiers used leather boots that laced up the front, much like really heavy hiking boots. They didn't keep the feet warm, were difficult to lace, and felt stiff. They were uncomfortable until "broken in," but they usually wore out shortly thereafter. Later, plastic boots hit the scene, but the early forms were still stiff and rubbed the foot uncomfortably.

Today's boots are usually made of a soft plastic called polyurethane. Although flexible, they still give the foot a firm grasp on the ski, making it easier to control. Ski boots have two parts: an inner boot that surrounds the foot to provide comfort, warmth, and support; and a firm outer shell that transmits power from your feet to your skis.

A ski boot should fit well, rest firmly on the foot without rubbing, and keep the foot warm. Only the toes should be able to wiggle; the rest of the foot should be held firmly in place. You should never have to wear more than one pair of socks to keep out the cold if a pair of boots fits correctly. Nonetheless, some skiers—including superstar slalom man Alberto Tomba—have decided that new-fangled boots with heating devices are the best thing going!

When you first try on a boot, you should wander around the store for at least half an hour with them on your feet. You won't be able to tell if anything rubs or if something is too tight unless you wear them for a while. What feels great at first may not be quite right. A good salesperson can adjust almost any problem to make the boot right for you.

Here's an important tip: After a day of skiing, remove the inner boot and let it air out. Your feet have probably sweated during the day, and if the boot isn't bone dry the next time you use it, your feet will be cold. Another thing to remember is not to put your boots in the trunk of the car when you ride to a ski area, or you'll start the day out with cold boots that will probably never get warm.

Ski poles are another important part of your gear. Skiers once used only a single pole, usually made of bamboo. In recent history, however, skiers have found that two poles greatly improve their balance and turning ability. Poles are now made of aluminum. They should be light but capable of taking pressure without bending or breaking.

Poles are held in place either with straps that go around your wrist or with "saber-style" grips that resemble the grip on a sword. Straps may be harder to put on and take off, but many advanced skiers prefer them. All poles have a circular basket about four inches across that is located two or three inches from the bottom. The basket keeps the pole from burying itself in deep snow when you plant it.

Clothing

Keeping warm is vital to having fun on the ski slopes. Being cold can ruin your enjoyment and your concentration, but more important, cold muscles and ligaments can be injured much more easily than warm ones. Fortunately, it isn't difficult to keep warm if you have the right ski wear. Skiers often dress in layers of clothes that trap pockets of warm air. As the day gets warmer or as exercise heats up the body, layers can be removed.

Start out with a pair of long underwear as the layer closest to the body. Long underwear traps heat and moves perspiration away from your body. Ski socks and a zipper turtleneck round out the bottom layer. Next, put on a pair of stretch pants, which are great for moderately cold days. They are flexible and water repellent. A ski sweater is next, but be careful not to choose one that is too thick, or it will restrict movement. Many skiers put on warm-up jackets, made of fabrics like GoreTex or synthetic fleece. These jackets provide light-weight warmth.

On colder days, you'll need a ski jacket or a parka, as well as a pair of warm-up pants. These garments have a thin layer of down or polyester filling that keeps you extra warm. Some skiers choose one-piece suits because it keeps air and snow out, a feature that is particularly important in powdery snow.

You will also need a good pair of gloves or mittens to keep your hands warm, as well as a hat. A warm hat is important, since much of your body heat can be lost through your head on cold days, leaving you vulnerable to illness. Goggles or sunglasses are very important to protect your eyes from the sun. In addition, the reflection of the sun on the snow can cause *snow blindness*, a sharp, burning sensation in the eyes.

The last thing you need is sunblock to protect your exposed skin from ultraviolet rays. You may think sun block is only for the beach, but the sun's rays are even more damaging in the mountains. Not only does the sunlight reflect back from the snow, but the high altitude places you a lot closer to the sun. You can get a severe burn if you don't apply sunscreen early and often, and remember to screen anything that is exposed, such as your ear lobes. Don't forget to protect your lips with lip balm as well—they burn very easily.

People who are prepared seldom have a bad time skiing—even on their first day out. Start with fitness, combine it with good ski equipment, and wear warm, comfortable ski clothing. This way, you're sure to think the sport is for you.

Learning to ski can feel extremely awkward at first, but for most people it takes less than a day to get the hang of it.

The Making of a Skier

The first time Jennifer went skiing, she couldn't believe how much her legs hurt by the end of the day. The next morning was horrible—her legs felt like two huge cement blocks, and every step made her wince.

"I had to go skiing again a week later because my parents had signed me up for these weekly ski lessons. At 6:30 in the morning, the very next Saturday, I was on the bus headed toward the ski area. I was really bummed. My friends, who were better skiers, were really into it. I just sat there wishing I was still in bed."

What happened that day surprised Jennifer. Not only did she remember what she had learned the week before, but she picked up on the new things her instructor told her. By the end of the day, she was making her way down the easy slopes with grace, smiling the whole way. This time, her muscles felt tired but not sore. The following week, Jennifer made her way down an intermediate slope—and it was only the third time she ever skied! "I probably didn't look all that hot, but I made it down," Jennifer remembers. "And I was psyched!"

If you're a beginner, don't be shy about taking a lesson. By learning just a few basics to control yourself and your skis, you'll have a much better time on the slopes.

Today Jennifer is a ski instructor. She spends her winters teaching children to ski. During the summer, she stays in shape with conditioning exercises and bike riding. "I'm in good shape," she says, "but the first day of the ski season always makes you a little sore. I'm not what you'd call a natural athlete, but I stay in shape all year so that I'm ready for the first snow fall."

Were you surprised that Jennifer could tackle intermediate slopes after just a few lessons? It isn't that unusual. After just one lesson, most skiers can handle simple turns and stops. It takes years, as well as many miles on the slopes, to become an expert. Fortunately, getting good enough to have fun can happen very quickly.

Although many children begin skiing shortly after they learn to walk, young people and adults can pick up the sport at any age. It doesn't matter when you start, and you don't have to be a world-class athlete. You can become a proficient enough skier to have fun and feel like you're truly talented. In addition, you don't have to live in one of the states that are famous for skiing, like Utah, Vermont, or Colorado. Michigan, for example, has 47 ski areas—more than any other state except New York.

Starting Out

Some experts suggest that people should try Nordic skiing first for a good introduction to the sport. Beginners who become familiar with skis on a flat or slightly hilly environment have the chance to feel what it's like to glide on snow, to climb with skis on, to turn, and to use ski poles. In addition, Nordic equipment is much lighter, making it easier to handle. You may find Nordic skiing is a good way to get comfortable with the sport before you try your hand at steeper slopes, but you may get hooked and decide that cross-country treks are for you!

Whether trying Nordic or Alpine, everyone should spend their first time on skis with a qualified instructor. Lessons give people the skills they need to make it down a mountain or through a valley without getting hurt. Once you learn certain techniques, skiing really isn't dangerous, but if you try the sport without learning any skills, you could be headed for disaster.

Instructors are trained not only to be great skiers, but to be good teachers as well. An instructor is able to tell if you're using the right equipment. He or she will run you through a series of drills before expecting you to go down a hill, making sure you're comfortable on your skis. He or she will be able to help you get on and off a chair lift without falling or getting your skis and poles tangled. Most of all, your instructor can teach you the skills you need to have fun with the sport.

When an instructor starts a lesson, his or her goal is to make sure the students are comfortable on their skis. You may be told to lift one ski up and turn it or walk around on flat terrain. You may be told to think of your boots and skis as nothing more than big feet, as if you'd been born with them and had to figure out how to get around.

Beginners don't try the ski lifts right away, so the next step will be to learn how to climb a little way up a hill so you can glide down it. The easiest way to climb is to *sidestep*. You'll stand across the fall line, that is, with your skis pointed sideways along the hill so that you don't start sliding down. Then, just like the word suggests, you'll take steps sideways up the hill, cutting the edges of your skis into the snow to prevent slipping. Your poles can help you balance and shift your weight.

Once you've climbed a little way up the hill, you'll probably learn straight running or schussing. Your instructor will teach you how to balance, how to stand on your skis, and how to slow down or stop. One method to control your speed is the "gliding" wedge (or snowplow), in which you place your skis in a "V" shape with the front tips almost touching. The inside edges of the skis are turned slightly into the snow, acting like grips to keep the skis from sliding. As you learn the wedge, you'll find that it is also a natural position in which to make a turn. A slightly wider wedge, called a "braking" wedge, will slow you down if you feel a little uncomfortable with your speed. Instructors prefer, though, that you control your speed with the gliding wedge and turns.

Ski areas almost always have ski instructors available to teach beginners, as well as improve the skills of more advanced athletes. *Professional Ski Instructors of America* (PSIA) is an organization that trains ski instructors. Many areas insist that instructors have PSIA training, and this usually ensures that a teacher has the know-how to teach beginners. These instructors use a specific method (called the American Teaching Method) that helps them plan lessons for their students.

For beginners, packages are usually available that include rental ski equipment, a two- or four-hour lesson, and a lift ticket. If you purchase such a package, you'll probably be part of a group class in which all the students are learning the basics. Group lessons are better than private lessons at this stage of the game because they are less expensive and a good way to make new friends who are sharing the same experience. Much can be learned by watching the techniques of other skiers.

The Lift

When your instructor feels that the class is ready, you'll take a chair lift up an easy hill (sometimes called a "bunny hill") for the first time. You'll probably be relieved, not scared, to try the lift because sidestepping up a hill on skis is a lot of work! You'll be told how to hold your poles as the chair approaches, and how to look over your shoulder and sit down slightly as the chair "scoops" you up. (At some smaller ski areas, you may ride a poma lift, a rope tow, or a T-bar, but these days, chair lifts are more common.)

Sit back and enjoy the view from the lift. It may stop while you're riding up the hill, but don't worry. It probably just means that someone needed a little extra help getting on or off, and the lift will start up again quickly.

Getting off a chair lift can be a bit more tricky, but your instructor will have told you what to do. For example, as you near the top, the tips of your skis should be grasped in one hand. As you approach the exit ramp, you ease slightly forward onto the edge of the chair. When your skis touch the exit ramp, you'll push off the chair and downward, as the chair moves up and behind you. You'll use your poles and the slight incline of the ramp to get out of the way before the next chair arrives at the ramp. Don't worry—if you fall, the lift operator at the top of the hill will stop the chair lift and assist you.

Your first impression, once you're off the chair lift, may be that the so-called bunny hill is a bit too steep for you to handle. It looks worse than it is when you're trying out your new knowledge for the first time, but by this time, you have the skills to make it down. In fact, by the end of the day, or at least by your next ski day, you'll want to try out more exciting terrain.

You have learned how to make wedge turns, how to straight run, and how to slow down and stop. You've also learned how to fall. If you ever feel like you're going too fast, a very simple way to stop is to just sit down! If you're straight running, sit down to the side; if you're traversing across the hill, sit down on the uphill side. Never fall on your knee or any other delicate part of your body—pretend you're sliding into home base. Remember that your rear end is padded, and landing on it is the best way to hit the snow.

All skiers fall on occasion, even the experts, but few falls end in injury. The world's top skiers sometimes even fall during an important race. It's part of the process. You'll find that as you lose your fear of falling, you'll try new things and become a better skier. If you hold back, you won't improve.

Many beginners classes are only half a day, usually in the morning. You'll break for lunch, and then you can take off and ski by yourself or with friends.

Expert downhill skiers love to explore the steeper runs, high above the beginner "bunny slopes" and warmth of the ski lodges.

Don't be afraid. You've learned enough to master the beginners' slopes. Your instructor will have explained the symbols on signs all around the ski area that show you how difficult a slope is. You'll want to stay on slopes with the green circle symbol—the easiest slopes. Blue squares indicate intermediate slopes, and black diamonds mean that a slope is for advanced skiers only. A double black diamond is reserved for the toughest of the tough—only experts need apply!

More Advanced Techniques

Once you've taken a lesson or two, you may think you can improve all by yourself, but there are still a lot of things you need to learn before you can head to the advanced slopes. You may want to ski a few days by yourself before taking another lesson, or you may want to spend your first four or five mornings in classes. Either way, lessons are vital to improve your skiing. Even expert skiers know that taking one or two lessons each season can improve their skills or help them break bad habits. Great skiers like downhill racer Marc Girardelli and slalom star Julie Parisien have coaches who help them improve their technique.

Using your ski poles properly helps you make sharper turns and keep your balance.

After making wedge turns for a while, you can start skiing down the slope a little faster and working on the *christy* or *stem christy*. This turn often happens naturally as skiers get a little practice, and it is the first step to more advanced turning. During a stem christy, the V-shaped wedge starts to come together as your inside leg starts to move toward the outside leg. The V shape is more narrow than that of the wedge, and as the turn is completed, the skis come together toward a parallel position. There are other turns you'll learn as you ski more slopes.

Later, skiers learn how to use their ski poles to help them turn. By planting them very lightly into the snow, you can help guide your body. Just like the turn signals on a car, you'll plant your left pole to turn left, your right pole to turn right, and then pull your skis into a parallel position and glide into the turn.

The ultimate goal of beginning skiers is to achieve the *parallel turn*. Here, the skis are never in the V position with which beginners are so comfortable.

Rather, as the skier glides down the slope, first on the right edges of the skis, then on the left, his or her skis are side by side. Parallel skiing looks great—it's one of the maneuvers that gives the sport such style. Once you know how to parallel, you'll probably be able to make it down most any hill.

Putting It Together

The world's top skiers don't have to think about whether their form is perfect, if they are using the correct edge to make a turn, or if their weight is distributed correctly. It is all second nature to them. After enough hours on the slopes, even relatively new skiers discover that they are skiing without thinking about every motion they make.

Think of it this way: When you learned to walk, you didn't know any fancy names for what you were doing. It just all came together. You might have fallen occasionally, but then you got back up and tried again. You didn't worry about what the correct form was, whether you should step with the right foot or the left, or which muscles to flex.

Our bodies learn how to do things from experience, that is, we *feel* how to perform a certain movement without having to think about it. From riding a horse to playing the piano, movement becomes instinctive with enough practice. Hearing all the rules, fancy names, and techniques of skiing may lead you to believe that learning the sport is difficult. Yet hundreds of thousands of skiers can't wait to hit the hills each winter. So get out on the slopes and try it for yourself. You're sure to find it really isn't tricky at all!

Downhill competitions feature lots of exciting, high-speed skiing.

The Competition

What is the reward for working hard and becoming an expert skier? First of all, the feeling of speeding down a tough hill is pretty satisfying, and being good at anything is a great way to build confidence. If you're looking for competition, however, you've definitely taken up the right sport. Alpine and Nordic skiing have exciting competitive events. Both are major international sports that attract men and women from around the globe.

Amateur skiers are those who do not win prize money or receive payment when they ski in competitions. In many sports, like tennis or football, being a professional and getting paid to do something you love is the name of the game. In skiing, however, the amateurs are the real stars. Professional skiers take part in exciting competitions in countries such as the United States, Japan, and Europe, but the most thrilling and important ski championships are for the amateurs.

Once an amateur becomes known as an unusually talented skier, he or she usually begins to race in important events. An American skier, for example, might be invited to join the U.S. Ski Team, which not only sponsors its own championships, but sends its best members to important international events.

The World Cup is today's most important amateur skiing championship for both Nordic and Alpine skiers. Skiers earn points according to how they finish in a race, and the individual who accumulates the most points wins the World Cup championship title. World Cup titles are awarded each year to the man and woman who have won the most points in a series of different races. Meets are held in countries around the world from December through March.

The World Ski Championships and the Winter Olympic Games are two other important venues for skiers, and events at these two championships are for both Nordic and Alpine skiers. The World Ski Championships are held every odd-numbered year; the Olympics are held every fourth even-numbered year.

Alpine Events

For skiers who love the feeling of going fast, there is *downhill racing.* This is a test of a person's ability to ski at high speeds. The average speed in a downhill race is 60 to 65 miles (97 to 105 kilometers) per hour—that's faster than the normal speed limit on United States highways! Control gates are placed along the downhill race course that direct skiers away from dangerous areas and force them to slow down. The gates are designated by two flags, and competitors must ski between them.

Many people think that the unbelievable speeds attained by downhill racers make this the most exciting of the Alpine events. Europeans have been very successful at this daredevil event. Only two American men have won the downhill title at the World Cup: Billy Johnson in 1984 and A.J. Kitt in 1992. Kitt has become a favorite at many recent events and is known not only as an excellent glider, but a man who can handle the turns while skiing at unbelievable speeds. Other great downhillers include two speedsters from Switzerland, Franz Heinzer and Daniel Mahrer.

American downhiller Kristin Krone has left her mark on the slopes, and Katja Seizinger of Germany had little trouble taking the 1992 World Cup downhill title. Taking charge of a challenging course that was 30 seconds longer than the average downhill World Cup course, Canadian Kerrin Lee-Gartner shot down the mountain to take the women's gold medal for downhill in the 1992 Olympics in Albertville, France.

The *slalom* is an event that tests a competitor's turning ability. The slalom course is marked by numbered gates placed at intervals of anywhere from .75 to 15 meters apart (.82 to 16.4 yards). Men's courses have 55 to 75 gates; women's courses have 45 to 60 gates. Skiers go down the course in a zig-zag fashion, turning at each gate. They must pass through the gates in order. The turns on such a course are tight, and the average speed is only about 25 miles per hour.

The *giant slalom* is a test of high-speed traversing, a sort of combination of the downhill race and the slalom. Giant slalom courses have fewer gates than slalom courses, and they are set a minimum of 5 meters (5.5 yards) apart. Since the gates are never as close together as they are on a slalom course, speeds are higher, averaging about 35 miles per hour.

Alpine events such as the slalom test a contestant's reflexes as the skier weaves between gates.

The *super giant slalom*, called the "Super G," is a cross between the downhill race and the giant slalom. Men's courses have 35 to 65 gates; women's have 30 to 50 gates. Gates are placed at intervals of 15 to 25 meters, and it is a longer—and faster—race than the other slalom events.

No racer today is more well known for slalom skills than Italian Alberto Tomba. A crowd-pleaser with some serious attitude, Tomba took the gold medal in the slalom in the 1988 Olympics and received the same honor for the giant slalom in both 1988 and 1992. At the start of 1992, he had won 25 World Cup races and went on to win both the slalom and the Super G title that year. Tomba doesn't ski downhill races, so you can be sure he scored very high in the slalom events to beat skiers who participated in more events than he did. To some fans of the sport, Tomba is a little arrogant, perhaps too impressed with himself. But the fact remains, Tomba is one of the world's finest skiers.

The *parallel slalom* is a race in which two or more small slalom courses are placed next to each other, usually about six or seven meters apart. Here, racers compete against each other to see who can run the course the fastest. *Combined competitions*, in which racers ski both a downhill and a slalom course, are another important event. To win the combined, a skier must be

Italy's Alberto Tomba is recognized as one of the finest giant slalom skiers ever.

good at both types of racing. Many skiers, however, excel only at one or the other—but not Austrian Petra Kronberger.

Kronberger is a star in today's Alpine racing world. In December of 1991, she became the first woman to win races in all four disciplines: downhill, slalom, giant slalom, and super G. Although she was injured fairly early in that season, she did well enough early on to win the year-long overall World Cup competition by more than 100 points—for the second year running. And guess what? She did it again in 1992! That's three World Cup championships in a row.

Nordic Events

Downhillers aren't the only skiers who can find stiff competition on the snow. Nordic fans have five events from which to choose.

Cross-country races take place on courses that are about one-third uphill, one-third downhill, and one-third flat. In the major meets, men's courses are 15, 30, and 50 kilometers (9.3, 18.6, and 31 miles); women's courses are 5, 10, and 20 kilometers (3.1, 6.2, and 12.4 miles). (Since ski racing is an international sport, the length of these courses is usually measured in the metric system.)

In most cross-country races, skiers begin at 30-second intervals. If there is a large number of people participating in the race, however, skiers sometimes begin two at a time on tracks that run parallel to each other. Skiers are timed to see how quickly they can complete the course, and the fastest person wins.

Cross-country relays are competitions in which teams race against each other. Like a relay event in track and field, each member of a cross-country team races an equal distance. One example is the four-person team that competes in the 40-kilometer (24.8 miles) men's relay in the Winter Olympics—each member of the team skis 10 kilometers (6.2 miles). One member starts, and at the completion of his ten miles, his teammate takes over. Each team's first skier starts at the same time, and the winning team is the one with the best time.

One of the big crowd pleasers at the Winter Olympics is *ski jumping*. In jumping competition, competitors slide down a steep track and then fly off a platform at the end. Skilled jumpers often fly for more than 300 feet (91 meters), making this event a thrilling spectator sport. Competitors receive points

That's Austrian skier Petra Kronberger "getting air" under her skis. Kronberger is one of the world's great skiers.

for both the style and length of their jump. An unbalanced or shaky landing can cost a jumper the win—even if he or she jumped farther than the competitors.

The *Nordic combined* is an event in which competitors race over a 15-kilometer (9.3 mile) course that includes three ski jumps. Skiers receive points for both.

The *biathlon* strikes many people as an unusual event, as it combines cross-country skiing and riflery. In the early days of skiing, however, men undoubtedly used skis to help them hunt during the winter months. The biathlon is usually 10 or 20 kilometers (6.2 or 12.4 miles) long. Targets are set up at different points along the course. Some targets are set so that skiers shoot standing up; others are set so skiers must shoot from a prone position (lying stomach down). Skiers are penalized for each target they miss, with seconds added to their race time. The individual who finishes the course in the shortest time wins. There is also a biathlon relay in which four skiers race 7.5 kilometers (4.5 miles) each.

Racing for the Rest of Us

Ski racing isn't just for international superstars. Less experienced skiers can try it, too. Once intermediate skiers have achieved a certain level of success, they can start running easy race courses. In fact, some instructors teach students how to clear gates in intermediate lessons.

Ski areas usually sponsor races for skiers of all abilities. *NASTAR*, the *National Standard Race*, offers an opportunity for skiers to get involved in recreational racing. These races are run all around the country. Each time a skier races in a NASTAR-sponsored race, he or she receives a handicap based on the time of the pacesetter, an advanced skier who runs the course. The pacesetter competes nationally to receive his or her handicap, so the system allows skiers to compare their handicap and their progress to skiers all around the country. An excellent handicap can qualify a less experienced skier for a medal from NASTAR, and national winners in various age categories are also eligible for a free trip to the U.S. Championships.

If you want to learn to race, talk to a ski school representative. There are undoubtedly classes available that will help you become familiar with the sport, and instructors can tell you about any upcoming races. Even if you don't expect to compete in the biggest events in the world, you can have a lot of fun competing against other skiers your age who share your interest. Who knows? Maybe you can move down a race course faster than anyone in a race, or score more points than any other slalom runner. You could be the next star of the slopes!

Hood or hat to keep in body heat and prevent sunburn.

Goggles help prevent snow blindness and reduce glare.

Warm gloves for gripping ski poles.

Ski poles should be appropriate length.

Snug-fitting ski boots with easy release from skis when you fall.

Once your skiing improves, you have so many ways to enjoy it: downhill, cross-country —even ski racing.

Freestyle Skiing

Freestyle is another incarnation of downhill skiing, and it has become so popular that it has inspired new events at the Winter Olympics. Freestyle skiing is also known as "hot-dogging." These creative skiers perform a variety of stunts like airborne somersaults and outrageous jumps. There are three types of freestyle skiing: aerial, mogul or bump, and ballet.

The most visually impressive form of freestyle skiing is *aerial*. Here, skiers swoop down steep hills or leap off large platforms to become airborne. While in the air they do dramatic spins, flips, and other moves before they land. They are judged both on the difficulty of the stunt and how well they executed it. The stunts look a little like the fancy maneuvers of gymnastics or diving.

Moguls are bumps on ski slopes, often very high and close together. Usually these bumps are formed naturally because many skiers turn in the same general place on a slope, which begins to pile snow into a mound. Expert slopes, where skiers speed down mountains, cutting many quick turns, tend to get the

The art of freestyle skiing has created a new competition category for the Winter Olympics.

most moguls. In addition, ski areas groom, or clean up, beginners' slopes to help prevent injuries to new skiers who can't handle tricky terrain. A lot of skiers, even some advanced skiers, don't like to ski moguls. Others believe they actually make skiing easier because they can help in executing a turn.

Skiers often make aerial turns on moguls. These occur when a skier glides over the top of a mogul and extends the legs in such a way that the body is propelled into the air. These turns not only look fun, but are essential for skiing the moguls.

Most advanced skiers can handle moguls, but not all of them are willing to strut their stuff in competition. That is reserved for the best "bump skiers" in the world. Today there are freestyle skiing events especially for mogul hounds. These fearless skiers face frighteningly steep slopes with lots of moguls. They speed down the run and jump off moguls while doing acrobatic maneuvers.

The final form of freestyle skiing is *ballet*. Here, skiers perform movements like those used in figure skating or gymnastics, usually on flat terrain. They perform routines set to music that include maneuvers like spins or somersaults.

Freestyle skiing has been compared to both gymnastics and ballet.

In recent years, there has been a lot of talk about *extreme skiing*, that is, skiing in places so dangerous or frightening that most people wouldn't even consider it. The word extreme means to go beyond the boundaries of moderation; it means the outermost or farthest point. In other words, extreme skiers go to drastic measures in search of never-before skied territory.

The French were the first extreme skiers. Because the Alps are famous for severe descents, virtually straight up and down, no one attempted to ski. Rock climbers loved the Alps for this very reason, using their pitons and ropes to ascend sheer mountain walls. Then one day, some daring mountaineers decided that if these reaches could be climbed, they could be skied as well. There was only one problem: If these skiers fell, they would die.

Americans have changed the sport somewhat. The United States version of extreme skiing is definitely daredevil and filled with exciting leaps off outrageous cliffs, but it is less related to radical mountaineering than to the acrobatics and aerials of freestyle skiers. American enthusiasts fly down a mountain, staying airborne for so long that their skis hardly seem necessary. They attack bumps and powder and steep inclines with gusto. It's risky, too, but American extreme is not nearly as dangerous as the European version. For the most part, these extremers are not facing death—only thrills and chills and a possible injury or two. While the Europeans were interested in finding a new route down a mountain, Americans are into having fun and leaving their tracks in some pretty amazing places.

One thing is for sure: Extreme skiing is not for everyone. You may be a good skier, but that doesn't mean you're ready for this type of snow challenge. For one thing, no matter how proficient a skier is, there is still one very real danger over which the person has no control: avalanche. When skiing out of bounds—areas where ski resorts are not available to groom and prepare slopes—avalanche is a common occurrence. Anyone who tries extreme skiing needs to know this is a real risk. Avalanches claim many lives every year.

Going the Distance

Just how far are ski bums willing to travel for a taste of snow? Recent trends indicate there are no limits. For example, *heliskiing* is becoming an incredibly popular trend. Tired of crowded slopes? Take a helicopter into a pristine landscape where no one else can go. Helicopters can take extremists into some pretty frightening territory, but it can also give expert skiers the chance to hit powder without a crowd or a long wait at the lift line.

Some skiers can't wait for the winter, so they head to the Southern Hemisphere to find the snow. Want to ski in August? Take a trip to Argentina! If that's a little beyond your price range, some North American ski areas, particularly in the western regions, stay open into July. Japan has taken it one step further: in that country, you can ski indoors on a 25-story tall, commercially built ski slope. You had better bring some cash, though. It costs $55 for just two hours. How can you tell who the real ski bums are? By how many months a year they hit the slopes!

Nordic News

What if you tried cross-country skiing and found you like it better than downhill? There are a lot of challenges for Nordic fans, too. Downhill skis are made for just that: going down hill. Since the bindings hold the heel as well as the toe to the ski, you are pretty much restricted to skiing in areas that have lifts. Nordic skiers, however, can ski into almost any snow-covered region, provided the terrain isn't too severe.

Why not take a ski trek? Europeans often spend several days touring the wilderness on skis, sleeping in huts built along ski trails. In the United States, you can make your way across Colorado's open country on trails specially designed for cross-country skiers. Or you can stay overnight in bunkhouses sprinkled around Maine's Baxter State Park while spending your days gliding through forests. In the California Sierra Nevadas, you can ski along scenic trails that offer overnight sleeping cabins.

For people interested in adventurous ski expeditions, *telemark skiing* presents a unique challenge. The sport combines cross-country and downhill skiing, and the telemarker makes it down steep hills with specially designed cross-country skis that allow turning in graceful arcs. With each turn, the knee bends deep, almost touching the ski. It looks a lot different than alpine skiing,

So what are you waiting for? Skiing is fun and easy to learn. All you need is some practice, some friends, and some powder!

and the technique is specialized to accommodate the different binding. Accomplished telemarkers can ski almost anywhere. They can get around with the basic Nordic techniques *and* they can face challenging downhill stretches. A telemark trek opens up a whole new world of places to try.

Something for Everyone

Since there are so many different ways to glide over snow, skiing is perfect for just about anyone looking for a way to enjoy winter. With the right attitude, a few hours spent with a good instructor, and decent equipment, you may find that skiing—whether Alpine or Nordic—is a sport you can enjoy for many fun-filled years.

So go hit the slopes!

Glossary

Alpine skiing. Skiing downhill. Alpine skiing is popular both as recreation and as a competitive sport.

Biathlon. A Nordic event that combines cross-country skiing with riflery.

Christy (stem christy). A more advanced turn than a wedge, when skis are placed in a more narrow "V" shape. Instead of edging the skis slightly inward, so that opposing edges are in the snow, corresponding edges are used. The skis are brought from a "V" position to a parallel one during the turn.

Combined competitions. A downhill event in which racers ski both a downhill and a slalom race.

Conditioning. Exercising in a variety of ways to achieve a certain level of fitness, especially in preparation for a specific sport.

Cross-country race. Nordic races in which skiers compete on a long course of up to 50 kilometers (31 miles). The individual who finishes with the best time wins.

Cross-country relay. A cross-country race in which teams race against each other. Each member of a team races an equal portion of the course; for example, on a 40-kilometer (24.8 mile) track, each member would race 10 kilometers (6.2 miles).

Cross-country skiing. A form of Nordic skiing in which skiers glide across flat or slightly hilly terrain, often over great distances.

Diagonal stride. The basic movement of cross-country skiing in which the skier moves one ski forward and then the other, as though jogging on skis.

Downhill racing. High-speed skiing run on a course with a strong vertical drop. Skiers reach speeds averaging 60 to 65 miles (97 to 104 kilometers) per hour.

Extreme skiing. A dangerous form of skiing that takes skiers into steep, unchartered places.

Fall line. The most direct route to the bottom of a slope.

Freestyle skiing. A form of downhill skiing in which skiers perform a variety of stunts.

Giant slalom. A ski race much like the slalom except that gates are placed at greater intervals, and there are usually fewer gates so that the average speed is higher.

Heliskiing. Taking a helicopter to ski in areas that cannot otherwise be reached.

Mogul. A mound of snow on a slope that is formed when many skiers turn in approximately the same place.

NASTAR (National Standard Race). An organization that sponsors races around the country for skiers at many different levels of ability.

Nordic combined. A Nordic event in which a competitor races over a course that includes ski jumps.

Nordic skiing. The term that refers to three specific forms of skiing: cross-country, telemarking, and ski jumping.

Parallel skiing. The ability to keep one's skis parallel at all times, even when making turns.

Parallel slalom. A ski race where two or more small slalom courses are placed next to each other so that racers compete against each other to see who can run the course the fastest.

Parallel turn (carved parallel). A difficult turn in which the skis maintain a parallel position through the completion of the turn.

Professional Ski Instructors of America (PSIA). An organization that trains ski instructors with advanced teaching methods to help students learn the sport quickly and safely.

Sidestepping. Placing the body at a 90-degree angle to the fall line (skis are pointed sideways on the hill to prevent sliding) and taking steps up the hill.

Ski jumping. A form of Nordic skiing in which individuals ski down a ramp and fly off a platform at the end, often leaping for distances of 300 feet (91 meters).

Slalom. A competitive ski race that tests a competitor's ability to turn at high speeds. The course has many gates that competitors must ski through in zig-zag fashion.

Snowboarding. A relatively new sport, snowboarders use a single board to slide down a mountain. It is a lot like surfing on snow.

Straight running (Schussing). Skiing straight down a hill without turning or stopping.

Super giant slalom. An event that is a cross between the downhill race and the giant slalom.

Telemark skiing. Skiing downhill with specially designed Nordic equipment.

Traversing. Skiing across a slope perpendicular to the fall line.

Wedge (snowplow). A turn in which skis are placed in a "V" position with the tips nearly touching and the edges tilted slightly inward. This turn can also be used to stop.

For Additional Information

Many ski videos are available now, both to rent or purchase. Some are thrilling films of expert skiers and snowboarders. Others offer instruction. A good one if you want to learn more about technique is "Learn to Ski" (Warner Home Video, 1986), produced by filmmaker Warren Miller.

To read more about skiing, take a look at the two most popular magazines about the sport, *SKI* and *Skiing*. Books that offer great advice include:

Skiing: Six Ways to Reach Your Skiing Potential, by Tim Petrick. New York: Time Inc., 1985.
Skiing by Jeremy Evans. Crestwood House, 1992.
Skiing by Donna Bailey. Raintree-SteckVaughan, 1990.

Index